Bartolome de las Casas
Champion of Indian Rights

by Dr. Fred Stopsky

Discovery Enterprises, Ltd.
Lowell, Massachusetts
1992

© Dr. Fred Stopsky, 1992

ISBN 1-878668-12-9 paperback edition
Library of Congress Catalog Card Number 92-71031

10   9   8   7   6   5   4   3   2   1

Printed in the United States of America

Subject Reference Guide:

Bartolome de las Casas – Biography
Native American Rights
Religion – Freedom of
Conquistadores – Opposition to
Catholicism – Conversion to
Christopher Columbus and Bartolome de las Casas

Illustrations

Cover design and illustrations by Leslie Carow.
Cover illustration is Ms. Carow's interpretation of a woodcut
from the New York Public Library.

Table of Contents

To Kate

for your patience and support

Introduction

Bartolome de las Casas is unknown to most Americans. There is an occasional reference to his work in a few history books. It is unfortunate that this courageous man who single-handedly defended the rights of Native Americans has disappeared from the pages of history. Instead, we learn about the conquistadores, whose sole purpose was to gain power and wealth even if it meant killing thousands of innocent people who got in their way.

From his youth in Spain, the life of Bartolome de las Casas was interwoven with that of Christopher Columbus. His uncle sailed on the first Columbus voyage, and his father accompanied Columbus on the second expedition. The Columbus family encouraged Las Casas to come to the New World, where they gave him land and Indian slaves. Las Casas never resolved this inner conflict. It was through Columbus that his family became wealthy; yet it was Columbus who introduced slavery and the brutal treatment of Indians.

Las Casas remained a loyal supporter of Columbus throughout his life, although he grew to hate the process Columbus began of destroying Native American life and cultures. The writings of Las Casas praise Columbus, but they also depict the horrors imposed upon Indians by the Admiral.

It is important to study the life of Las Casas if we wish to better understand the rich cultural life of Indians in the Americas. Bishop las Casas respected the beliefs and values of Indians. He attempted to understand their cultures and learn about their history. He did not view them as "savages" fit only to serve the conquerors. He was an unusual person for this period because he believed Native Americans were equal in ability to the Spaniards.

His belief in the idea that all humans had natural rights to freedom was unusual for that era in human history. Few agreed with him that Native Americans had a right to rule themselves and practice their cultural beliefs. If Indians had natural rights, it was a short step to advocate these same rights for all humans.

Las Casas' struggle to persuade the Catholic Church and the Spanish monarchy that Indians were entitled to freedom raised issues that are still important today. He was among the few men who openly supported freedom of religion at a time when the Inquisition was torturing and burning people who uttered such thoughts. He made his church rethink its ideas about religious freedom. He was a man of the twentieth century, living in the sixteenth.

The life of Bartolome de las Casas has some interesting insights for young people. He made terrible mistakes early in life. He owned Indians and used them to obtain wealth. He turned a deaf ear to those opposing slavery. He observed horrible crimes and remained silent. Perhaps the most terrible mistake of his early life was to urge the introduction of slaves from Africa.

Why study about a man who made mistakes? The answer is clear: Bartolome de las Casas looked inside himself, discovered aspects of his life he did not like, and changed. He is proof that anyone can correct a mistake. His life shows that it is not the mistakes we make, but the manner in which we correct them that is important.

There are reasons we should remember this gallant figure from the sixteenth century. He wrote an important history book, The History of the Indies. Among other things, this book contains names, dates, and factual accounts of how the Spanish brutalized Native Americans.

His life is the story of a crusader for freedom. He never totally achieved what he set out to do. He never was able to halt the persecution of Indians. But, he began the work of changing Spanish attitudes toward Indians. Las Casas had only two titles in the ninety-two years of his life: he was Bishop of Chiapa and Protector of All the Indians of the Indies. He realized it was not the titles that counted, but taking a stand for human rights.

Chapter 1

The Early Years

Bartolome and his father walked along the docks. It was a sunlit day in August, and a gentle breeze was on their faces. "See, father, there is uncle waving to us." A bearded man on the deck of a small sailing ship waved eagerly. Bartolome turned to his father: "Do you think they will actually be able to reach Asia by sailing west?"

His father shook his head. "I don't know my son, I really don't know. Come, let us kneel and pray for the safe return of your uncle. He is embarking on a dangerous and long journey into the unknown."

A wind ruffled the sails, and the ship moved forward. Bartolome could see his uncle hanging on to the rigging of the Santa Maria as it sailed out of Palos harbor in Spain.

Father and son got on their mules and headed home to Seville. They talked about the voyage as they rode across the dry flat plains of Spain. "Everything depends upon the wisdom of the leader of this expedition," said his father. "This Christopher Columbus is unknown to most people. I hope he can guide the ships to Asia."

Pedro de las Casas had mixed feelings about the voyage to Asia. He wanted to go with his brother, but concern for his family held him back. "I wonder if I should have gone. Columbus promised that all who went with him would return as wealthy men. I just could not leave at this time when you are preparing to enter the University of

Salamanca. If the trip is successful, then I will go the next time."

Bartolome de las Casas was born in Seville in 1474. His grandparents were probably Jewish. A great number of Jews converted to Christianity under pressure from the Spanish government. His father, Pedro, was a merchant who was continually in debt. His mother was a quiet woman who insisted that Bartolome and his two sisters behave themselves. She ran the house with a firm hand.

Bartolome had a happy childhood in Seville. The city was an important seaport which drew ships and trade from all parts of the Mediterranean Sea. The children of Seville were exposed to people from many countries. It was common to hear a sailor tell an interested crowd about his adventures among the Arabs or about a voyage along the African coast. The spirit of adventure and exploration was in the air.

Bartolome was a serious child who was deeply religious. He often went to church with his mother. He sat in the quiet, dark, chilly church feeling inspired by the ceremonies conducted by priests. "Mother," he said one day, "I have decided to become a priest. I want to study religious law at the University of Salamanca."

Bartolome entered law school in the fall of 1492, a few months after his uncle left with Christopher Columbus to seek a western water route to Asia. College life was very relaxed. Students spent a great deal of time in inns where they talked, drank, and sang. Sometimes, they argued about the ideas of Columbus.

"It is impossible to reach Asia by sailing west," said one student. "It is too far away." Bartolome defended Columbus. "My uncle told me that Columbus has a map which proves Asia is only about 3,400 miles away. It can be reached by ship."

Days passed. Weeks passed. Months passed. The students stopped talking about Columbus. Most people assumed he had died somewhere on the open seas. Bartolome worried about his studies and exams. The dream of reaching Asia disappeared with the onset of winter.

One day in March, 1493, Bartolome was on his way to class when he heard shouting in the street. A small crowd was gathered around a man who was gasping for breath after his long ride. "Columbus is back! Columbus has returned!" he shouted. "He has come back with enormous riches and he even brought back people who live in the land of the Indies."

Bartolome was an excited spectator on the day Christopher Columbus entered Seville. He ran to his uncle and hugged him with joy. He stepped back and saw several shivering "Indians" who looked at the crowd in bewilderment.

"Bartolome, Bartolome," laughed his uncle, "see what I brought you. Here is a belt of fine gold, some Indian masks, and a red bird they call a parrot. I even brought you a rubber ball that the Indian children play with."

Years later when Bartolome was an old man, he often said that the most amazing sight to him on that historic day was the rubber ball. It was as large as a jug and bounced twice as high as balls used by Bartolome and his friends when they played soccer. The ball had been made from the juice of a rubber tree. Bartolome was among the first people of Europe to own a rubber ball.

Later that night, Bartolome and his family listened in wonder as his uncle told tales about the lands lying near the Asian continent. He described land so fertile anything could grow in its rich soil. He told them about men and women who walked around without any clothes. "They are heathens, they do not understand anything at all about religion. Bartolome, they need young priests to go among them and bring the truth of Christianity."

"Is it safe in this new land?" asked Bartolome. His uncle smiled. "Well, there are people called the Caribs who wage war, and then eat their captives, but most of the Indians are generous and kind."

Bartolome's father was excited about the new lands. He went to see Admiral Columbus and begged permission to go on the next voyage to the new world. Columbus took a liking to Pedro de las Casas and signed him on for his second expedition which would leave later that year.

Seville became a beehive of activity as preparations were made for the voyage. Stores and provisions were placed on the ships. Many people volunteered to go along as colonists. Lost in the excitement was any concern for the Indians who had been taken from their homes and brought to Spain. Many became ill, and a few died.

One day, the entire city heard shouts and hurrahs welcoming the arrival of Queen Isabella and King Ferdinand. The monarchs came to Seville to personally wish the crew a bon voyage. The men stood at attention on the ships as Queen Isabella presented crimson sashes to the captains. Then, sailors and spectators knelt in prayer. The explorers took an oath of loyalty to the King and Queen. Bartolome was proud that his father would play a role in this great adventure.

Months passed. Years passed. There was no word from his father. Bartolome made frequent trips to the port of Las Muelas hoping a ship from the West Indies would bring news about his father and his uncle. He met sailors who had been to the Indies. They told tales about strange creatures and dangerous fights with Indians, but none had news of his father.

Bartolome was in Las Muelas in December,1496 when suddenly, on the horizon, he saw five ships enter the harbor. He knew that his father and uncle were on the ships.

He was relieved. Soon, he could see their faces on the deck of a ship.

"Father, father," he shouted, "How were things in the Indies?" His father's face was wracked with fatigue. "My son, we had great adventures, but we did not find great wealth. However, I did bring back an Indian boy who will be your slave."

Bartolome was among the first people in Europe to have an Indian for a slave. He was kind to the boy, and they became friends. Bartolome did not like the idea of owning a slave so he freed the youth, and arranged that the boy could return to the West Indies.

Bartolome's father was proud that his son would become a priest. "Bartolome, I think you would do well to seek your fortune in the Indies. It is a land bursting with riches. There is great need for settlers and new towns. Come with me on my next voyage."

After a few days, Bartolome made his decision. "I will go with you, father. I am anxious to visit new places and see new things. Columbus is a great man, and I want to play a part in his discoveries. I want to help make Spain the greatest nation in the world."

Chapter 2

In the New World

Bartolome and his father sailed for the West Indies in February, 1502. They were part of a fleet of ships sailing to the West Indies which Columbus still believed was close to the Asian continent. Bartolome stood on the deck watching the beautiful Spanish countryside slowly disappear in the distance. Ovando, captain of the expedition, was on his way to the West Indies to replace Christopher Columbus as governor.

After a difficult two-month journey, Bartolome's boat reached the island of Santo Domingo in 1502. He stepped ashore almost ten years after Christopher Columbus had first reached the West Indies. He was shocked to see the conditions on the island. Exhausted Indians walked slowly through the streets. Many were close to death due to illnesses brought over by the Europeans. The Spanish colonists had only one thought on their minds, and that was to find gold.

Bartolome de las Casas was a typical Spanish settler. He regarded the Indians with pity, but his mind was also on finding a way to gain wealth. There was much talk about the importance of bringing Christianity to the Indians, but little was done about it. Bartolome obtained a farm, and was given Indians to work the land for him. Years later, he recalled with shame his early attitude towards Indians.

Bartolome settled down to the life of a landowner. He built a house, expanded his fields, and forced more Indians to

9

work his land. Little thought was given to improving the lives of Indians or their families. One day another settler asked him to go along on a trip. "We are going to teach the Indians a lesson. Come along and see the fun."

The Spanish force marched into the interior of the island of Cuba. Several Indian chiefs agreed to meet with the Spanish and offered their visitors food and drink. Ovando persuaded the Indians to enter a house, then placed armed men around it to "keep anyone from leaving; they set fire to the house burning alive all those kings who, together with the wood and straw, were soon turned into burning embers."

Las Casas watched the Spanish horsemen spearing as "many Indians as they could while the soldiers on foot ripped bellies open." He was horrified that the soldiers shoved lances into the bodies of young children and babies. But, Las Casas did nothing to halt the massacre; he just watched.

He made several trips into the interior to meet and talk with Indians. He met the boy who had once been his slave. "Bartolome," said the young man, "are you proud of your Spanish countrymen? You once told me to become a Christian. Do you want me to behave like these men of your faith who kill innocent women and children?"

Bartolome was confused. He knew it was against Christian principles to kill the innocent. He wondered how he could think of becoming a priest and remain quiet in the face of these massacres. What exactly was he doing about bringing Christianity to the Indians? On the other hand, his father and uncle supported the destruction of Indians. They urged him to make money.

The arrival of Diego Columbus as governor helped the family of Las Casas. The son of Christopher Columbus liked the family, and rewarded Bartolome with large grants of land and Indians to work for him. Bartolome and his father became increasingly wealthy.

10

After several years as a planter, Bartolome de las Casas decided to become a priest. He was the first priest to be ordained in the New World. Las Casas celebrated his first public mass in 1512. It was a joyous celebration, and the settlers showered him with gold coins. They regarded Las Casas as a priest who would support their actions against the Indians. He never criticised them for attacking Indian villages. His reward was more land and more Indians.

Las Casas was a wealthy man with large investments in land, cattle, and mining. He had dozens of Indians to do his work. But, something began to bother him. He could not accept that the Indians were being killed or worked to death. He visited villages and always heard the same plea, "We are hungry, we are hungry, please help us." The Indians complained that men were worked to death in the mines, while the women and children starved.

More and more the visits bothered his conscience. He believed in Christianity, yet he was part of a conquering force that killed thousands of people. He could not get rid of the sight of otherwise decent Spanish men laughing as they crushed Indian babies beneath the hoofs of their horses. Bartolome wondered if he was a sinner. Was the entire Spanish invasion a sin?

One day Bartolome visited a newly arrived group of Dominican priests and was introduced to Father Antonio Montesino. Father Montesino was distraught at the manner in which Spanish settlers treated the Indians. "I will preach a mass this Sunday which urges our people to cease oppressing Indians." The next Sunday Las Casas heard a powerful sermon:

You are living in deadly sin for the atrocities
you tyrannically impose on these innocent
people. Tell me, what right you have to
enslave them? What authority did you use
to make war against them who lived at peace
on their territories, killing them cruelly with
methods never before heard of? And, why
don't you look after their spiritual health, so
that they should come to know God, and that
they should be baptized, and that they should
hear Mass and keep the Holy Days? Aren't
they human beings?

The congregation was shocked. This was the first
public attack upon the Spanish conquistadores. It was the first
open defense of Indians. That night, colonists met at the
house of an angry Diego Columbus.

"Governor, you must demand that Father Montesino
apologize for his slander against us. Ship all these Dominican
priests back to Spain where they belong. We have no use for
disloyal Spanish in our midst." The head of the Dominican
Order agreed to have Father Montesino apologize on the
following Sunday.

The entire town came to church to hear the apology.
Father Montesino strode to the pulpit, and in a firm voice said:
"I shall repeat my knowledge and my truth and I will show my
words of last Sunday that so embittered you to be true." He
then listed example after example of mistreatment and killing
of Indians.

The settlers stormed from the church and again
marched to the house of the governor. "Let us draft a
statement to King Ferdinand himself demanding recall of this
lying priest. We don't need traitors around here to help these
lying murderous Indians."

12

There were few supporters for Indian rights at the court of King Ferdinand. His advisors rejected the pleas of the Dominicans that the Indians be protected against the settlers. The Dominicans were allowed to remain, but were forbidden to interfere with attacks upon Indians. Bartolome de las Casas remained silent during the controversy. He still identified with Spanish colonists, and thought owning Indian slaves was quite normal.

King Ferdinand of Spain, reprinted from The Letter of Columbus on the Discovery of America, Trustees of the Lenox Library, N.Y. 1892.

Chapter 3

A Change of Heart

One day Las Casas was in the study reading the Bible, when his eye was struck by a passage in the thirty-fourth chapter of Ecclesiasticus: "Stained is the offering of him that sacrificeth from a thing wrongfully gotten." He thought about Father Montesino. He thought about how he had gotten his own wealth from the sweat and toil of slaves!

Suddenly, a veil was removed. Las Casas knew what he must do in order to be a good Christian. Bartolome visited his old friend, Governor Diego Columbus. "Sir, I have decided that it is impossible to be a devout Christian and own slaves. I have obtained wealth through wrongful means by using the labor of innocent Indians. I shall sell my lands and use the money to aid the Indians. I shall devote the remainder of my life to helping these unfortunate people."

The Governor urged him to reconsider, but Las Casas was firm in his belief that the oppression of Indians must cease. "I shall walk a new path from now on; one that leads to freedom for Indians."

Las Casas joined forces with the Dominicans and began a series of Sunday sermons aimed at defending the rights of Indians. His former friends were furious at what they considered to be an act of betrayal. They sat in stony silence as the former slave holder preached freedom for Indians. He met icy stares of hatred as he walked in town.

Las Casas formed new friendships with members of the clergy who wanted to end slavery. He joined them in their

14

trips across Cuba to defend the rights of the Indians. Colonists threw stones at them and yelled curses. "We don't want your kind around here! Go back to Spain, and take these thieving savages with you. See if the people of Spain want Indians living in their towns."

Las Casas decided it might be necessary to see the King and urge him to reconsider Spain's policies toward the Indians. He met with fellow reformer, Father Pedro de Cordoba. "Bartolome," said his colleague, "I know you want to help the Indians, but I doubt if you will find support among the advisors to the King."

"Father," replied Bartolome, "I shall try in every way I can, and will undergo all the labor necessary to accomplish the goal I have embarked upon, and I hope Our Lord will aid me; but should I not attain it, I will have done what I ought as a Christian; and may your Reverence commend me to God, now and always."

Las Casas sailed for Spain in September, 1515.

Chapter 4

The Fight Begins

King Charles was now the ruler of Spain. That role enabled him to claim a portion of all wealth coming from the New World. The King allowed "encomiendas" to be created. The encomienda system gave land to Spanish settlers, and gave them the right to enslave Indians to farm the land. The end of slavery would reduce his revenues. Las Casas realized it would be difficult to convince him that a new system was needed.

The King also benefitted from the use of Indians in mining. Columbus had introduced the idea that Indians should work in the mines, with a portion of all gold and silver extracted to be given to the King of Spain. Las Casas had to try to persuade the monarch to give up a major source of his wealth.

Before approaching the King, Las Casas went to the Colegio de San Gregorio to study. He wanted to find reasons why under church law Indian slavery was illegal. He emphasized to the priests at the college the vital need to quickly end slavery. "We believe that when Columbus reached the West Indies, about one million Indians lived in the area. Today, I doubt if more than 25,000 are still alive. If we don't act soon, all the Indians will be gone."

His family became aware that Bartolome had changed. He no longer desired wealth obtained at the expense of his fellow man. He talked only about the plight of the Indians and the need to help them gain freedom.

The Spanish clergy was divided over the best way to handle the question of freedom for Indians. Many agreed with the encomienda system because they considered Indians savages who should be enslaved and re-educated. A smaller number of priests wanted Indian freedom. Las Casas and his allies were powerless against the threat of Spanish colonists in the New World to rebel if the King ended slavery.

The time had come for Las Casas to come forward. He was not a famous man and he lacked connections at the court. Yet, he spoke boldly. "Your Highness, I am only a humble priest, but I know that the Church must take a strong stand against slavery. If you don't stop this horrible system, thousands more Indians will die."

"Father Bartolome," said the King, "I am King to all my subjects, including Indians. How can we aid the Indians without angering settlers in the New World?"

"Sire, I believe there is a way out of this problem. I propose that we recruit a new group of settlers. They would be given large grants of land, but, in exchange, they would agree to train and educate Indians as farmers. After a certain number of years, the Indians would be given their freedom and land. In the meantime, priests would educate the Indians in the ideas of the Christian faith. The Indians would be peacefully converted to Christianity, and you would receive a portion of all wealth created by these Indian farmers."

The King agreed to this proposal if Las Casas could find enough settlers to venture to the New World under these conditions. Now, Las Casas would have to convince Spanish settlers to give up their bias against Indians and treat them on equal terms.

He spent two years traveling throughout Spain seeking people interested in going to the New World who would treat Indians in a decent manner. Las Casas finally gathered two hundred sympathetic Spaniards to sail for the

Americas. The Dominican order agreed to sponsor the project and set up an outpost on the coast of South America. The word "America" came from the voyages and writings of Amerigo Vespucci. It gradually became used by the Spanish to refer to the New World.

Local Spanish colonists were furious to learn about the project. They attacked Indian villages to show their disappointment. The Indians fought back, and attacked the Dominican outpost. Spanish officials turned a blind eye to criminal raids on the Indians. In fact, they encouraged the settlers to raid villages, seize Indians as slaves, and give them liquor to cloud their minds and force them to submit.

Las Casas tried to reason with the officials and settlers. "This is a wonderful chance for the Spanish and Indians to cooperate with one another. We can bring the word of Christianity to the Indian people in a joyous and peaceful manner." The Spanish officials scoffed at his idea. They wanted to prove to King Charles that peace was impossible with the Indians.

The project came to a sad end in 1522. The Indians fought back against continual raids on their villages. In one of their own attacks, they burned down the Dominican mission. The priests escaped, but peaceful relations with Indians was at an end.

Las Casas, broken hearted, returned to Santo Domingo. He walked along the seashore and in the forest thinking about his failure to end the tyranny against the Indians. "What did I do wrong?" he wondered. "Was my mistake telling the King he would make a profit by acting decently toward the Indians? Should I have appealed to his sense of honor as a good Christian rather than link humane treatment with the potential for profit?"

Las Casas came to the conclusion he had made Spanish greed more important than the spiritual needs of the

Indians. He felt despair at his inability to peacefully convert the Indians to Christianity.

His torment was so great that he entered a Dominican monastery on Santo Domingo, where he spent the decade from 1520 - 1530. "The cleric," he wrote about himself, "now a friar, Fray Bartolome de las Casas, slept as it seems for some years." He used the time to reflect, read, and study.

In the quiet of the monastery, Las Casas began work on an important historical piece, <u>History of the Indies</u>. This book is considered the most important document written in the sixteenth century that defends Indian rights. He created a new plan to help Indians by placing priests in charge of educating them in farming. However, he was unable to get support for this idea.

Las Casas finally broke his silence with a letter to the King. He described the terrible treatment of the Indians by Spanish settlers. Once again he pleaded for help to prevent the wiping out of the entire Indian population.

His concern for Indians got the better of his judgment. Las Casas urged the King to import slaves from Africa to populate the islands, and free the Indians. He wanted several hundred African slaves placed on each island so Indians would be freed and allowed to live under decent conditions.

Las Casas regretted this suggestion for the rest of his life. He felt tremendous remorse for his part in making Africans into slaves. His concern for the Indians was so great that it had led him into a proposal that would inflict horror upon other innocent humans.

Chapter 5

Struggling for Peaceful Conversion

While in Santo Domingo Las Casas had a chance to show his concern for Indians during the rebellion of Enriquillo. Enriquillo was an Indian who was educated by Franciscan monks, became a Catholic, and was married in the church. He returned to his village and got a job with a local landowner.

One day while Enriquillo was at work, the Spanish landowner attacked Enriquillo's wife. Enriquillo protested to the Spanish authorities, but they beat him, and threw him in jail. Enriquillo escaped and fled to the mountains with some friends. Spanish troops attempted to capture him, but Enriquillo defeated them time after time.

News of his success against the Spanish spread throughout the island. Hundreds of Indians joined his guerilla band. Enriquillo insisted on several rules of behavior among his troops. They were only to kill Spanish in self defense. Captured Spanish soldiers were to be disarmed and returned home. Indian women and children were to be taken to mountainous areas where they could live in safety.

Enriquillo's army controlled a large area of Hispaniola for several years. The Spanish attempted to make peace, but Enriquillo suspected that their offers were not sincere. Las Casas agreed to leave the monastery and meet with Enriquillo to arrange peace.

"Don Enrique," said Las Casas at their meeting. "I have come to hear confessions from my Catholic brothers and

sisters, and to work out an agreement to end this warfare." The
two men embraced. "Father Bartolome," replied Enrique, "you
are among the few Spanish we trust. You treat us as equals to
any Catholic. Let us have peace and end the war."

After mediating the Enriquillo revolt, Las Casas
decided it was time to leave the monastery. "I have lived in
the West Indies for nearly thirty years, and have achieved little
success in aiding my Indian brothers and sisters," he told the
head of the monastery. "I have decided to go to Central
America where Cortes recently defeated the Aztecs. I believe
there is much work in that area of the world. Perhaps, we can
create bonds of equality between Spaniard and Indian."

In 1519 Hernan Cortes led an army which defeated and
killed Montezuma, King of the Aztecs. The Spanish took
over the Aztec empire, and stripped the land of its wealth.
Like the Indians in the Caribbean, the Aztecs suffered terribly
from Spanish oppression. It is estimated that within thirty
years only six million Aztecs survived of the twenty-five
million whom Cortes had conquered.

Las Casas reached Central America about fifteen years
after the Cortes conquest. He found Nicaragua in 1535 to be a
devastated region. Thousands of Indians had been enslaved by
their Spanish conquerors. Las Casas visited deserted villages
where only the elderly remained.

Ten years in the monastery did not quiet the fiery
temper of Las Casas. He visited the Governor of Nicaragua
and condemned the Spaniards' attacks upon Indians. "Your
Excellency, conditions in this region are deplorable. Our
mission as Christians is to aid people to discover the truth of
our faith. All people are brothers and sisters before God. You
must cease these cruel attacks and halt the enslavement of
Indians."

"Father Bartolome, you tend to souls and I will tend
to wealth. Spain needs gold to become powerful and fight

21

against its enemies. The King did not send us out here only to convert heathens. He wants us to make Spain a wealthy and powerful nation."

"Then, you leave me no option but to refuse to hear confessions of any Spanish soldiers who engage in seizing people for slavery."

The Governor was furious and demanded that the superiors of Las Casas banish him from Nicaragua.

Las Casas and several other priests went to the neighboring area of Guatemala. The Indians were waging fierce resistance to the Spanish invasion. In fact, the interior of Guatemala was known as "Tuzulutlan" or "The Land of War." Las Casas persuaded the Spanish Governor to halt slave raids and give the priests a chance to restore peace to the land.

Tuzulutlan was an area containing mountains, intersected by rivers, and lost amidst dense forests. The Indians of the region hated the Spanish and were determined to protect their freedom. Las Casas faced a problem: how could he convince the Indians that friendship, not war, was his goal?

The priests spent many anxious nights discussing the situation until they came up with a novel approach. Las Casas made friends with several Indian merchants who traded with inhabitants of Tuzulutlan. He peacefully converted these merchants to Christianity. Then, the priests taught the merchants how to spread the message of Christianity through singing songs! They even set verse to music using Indian musical instruments as accompaniment.

The newly converted Christian Indian merchants set out through the dense forests. Deeper and deeper they wound into the interior. They came to a town on the edge of Tuzulutlan which was an important trading center. That night, the Indian merchants gave a concert. They sang and played music. The inhabitants of Tuzulutlan were enchanted by the music and the message of the songs. They asked questions and discussed the meaning of Christianity with the merchants. The next day they agreed to allow Las Casas to build a church in their town.

A short time later Las Casas and his fellow priests arrived in the town. Indians came from all parts of the interior to hear the singing priests. Many were converted to Christianity and sent back to spread the word. This experiment in peaceful conversion was in sharp contrast to the usual Spanish method of forcing religion upon people. The sword of war was put aside and replaced with music, laughter, and poetry.

News of peaceful Spanish spread among the Indians living in the land of war. Bands of people walked through the forests to find the priests of peace. Las Casas had churches built throughout the area. He converted a large number of Indians. Las Casas was then able to bring together the leaders of the Indians and Spanish officials to negotiate an end to the war and slave raids.

In the midst of his successful work to end the bloody war, Las Casas was called to Mexico City for an important meeting. He attended a conference aimed at improving the work of missionaries in the New World. Unfortunately, while he was gone, new priests arrived in Tuzulutlan. They backed Spanish colonists who wanted to restore war and slave raids. The plan for peaceful conversion collapsed, and warfare resumed.

Las Casas spent the following two years from 1538 to 1540 in Mexico. He became involved in a fierce debate about the best way to convert Indians. Some priests wanted large numbers of Indians converted all at once. Las Casas preferred encouraging individuals to make a commitment to Christianity.

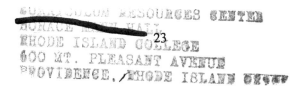

He decided to write a book urging peaceful conversion of Indians. Las Casas recognized that the Indians were not heathens who lacked spiritual values. The majority of religious leaders in Spain were ignorant about the culture of Indians. Las Casas presented evidence in his book to prove that Indians were intelligent beings, whose culture contained advanced ideas in the arts and science. He emphasized that the Spanish had encountered important civilizations in the Americas, but had destroyed them without seeking to understand their values or beliefs.

His book was a powerful argument against use of war to make people adopt Christianity. He pointed out that Indians had usually welcomed Christians until they were attacked. Several priests in Mexico City agreed with him that peaceful conversion was important, but leaders of the church failed to support his views.

Las Casas grew weary from arguing with religious leaders who failed to see the need for peace between Spaniards and Indians. There were too many powerful groups in the New World who backed Indian slavery. Las Casas decided he must return to Spain and convince the monarchy to support the end of Indian slavery once and for all.

Chapter 6

Defender of the Indians

Las Casas discovered after arriving in Spain that his reports concerning mistreatment of Indians had aroused the conscience of many members of the clergy. His opponents still had the ear of the King, but Las Casas had new support to advocate change.

Bartolome de las Casas supported ideas that were not popular in his generation. He believed all humans originally were free, having been given that right directly from God. All people had a right to freely practice their religion. This meant the Catholic Church should not use force nor should it impose its views upon any people.

Las Casas directly addressed the issue of the Pope's role in the New World. He argued that the Pope could teach non-Christians about Christianity, but he lacked authority to take away their land, property or liberty. However, the Pope could place Christian kings in charge of non-Christian lands for the purpose of encouraging the peaceful spread of Christianity.

Las Casas argued that the King of Spain had a responsibility to protect the Indians' right to choose to become Christians or to practice their own religious beliefs. He wanted to end the encomienda system which placed Indians under control of Spanish colonists. Las Casas suggested that the King control the Indians and that he send priests to peacefully convert them.

Father Las Casas angered many Spanish people by his strong defense of Indian rights. He wanted to restore all land and property taken forcibly from Indians. He demanded that gold or treasures stolen from Indians be returned, down to the last penny. These were fighting words to the Spanish conquerors who took whatever they desired from the Indians.

Las Casas went to the court of King Charles V in 1541. He had been away from Spain for over twenty years. His last appearance had been as an unknown priest from the West Indies. This time, he was warmly embraced by friendly priests who supported his work in defending Indian rights.

The King was advised in deciding laws for the New World by a group known as the Council of the Indies. The Council prepared laws and rules to govern the Spanish possessions in the Americas. Las Casas appeared before the Council and described to the members brutality toward the Indians. He cited example after example of cruelty, torture, killing, burning, looting, whippings, and forced conversions.

Priests on the Council were shocked at his account. They ordered a study to be made about conditions in the New World, and asked Las Casas to write suggestions for how laws should be changed.

A joyous Las Casas walked away from the chambers of the Council into the bright Barcelona sunshine. He wandered around the city, watched lovers stroll hand-in-hand, and listened to the laughter of children. "I wonder," he thought, "how such loving people can become transformed into viscious killers once they step ashore in the New World. Why can't they see that Indians have children who are entitled to love and freedom?"

That night, Las Casas knelt in prayer with his fellow priests. He was sixty - eight years old. It had been fifty years since his uncle had first sailed with Columbus to the New World. He remembered his uncle's description of the beauty and wonder of the West Indies, and the gentleness and kindness of the people. The young priests sat in awe listening to his stories of faraway places and unusual sights. They were proud a member of the clergy had stood up to the most powerful people in Spain in order to defend the rights of oppressed humans.

The Council of the Indies reviewed the evidence given by Las Casas and others. In November, 1542, the Council made sweeping recommendations to King Charles for a total change in policy toward the Indians. The King issued the New Laws of 1542 which included nearly every idea presented by Las Casas to the Council. The laws said:

1. The taking of Indians as slaves is forbidden.
2. No Indian should be compelled to work against his will.
3. Indians have to be paid fair wages for their work.
4. All encomiendas held by government officials or the clergy are to be ended. Their Indians are to be placed directly under the control of the crown.
5. No future private encomiendas are to be granted. At the death of current holders of encomiendas, Indians will be placed directly under control of the crown.
6. All Indians placed directly under control of the crown are to be treated decently and persuasion is to be used to make them Christians.

"At last, we have laws to back our efforts to protect the Indians," he told his fellow priests. "However, the fight has just begun. Spanish officials and colonists in the New World will attempt to sabotage these laws. We will need new officials sent out to ensure the laws are carried out in practice."

The Council of the Indies listened respectfully to Las Casas and his pleas for new officials. However, they also received strong protests from Spanish colonists in the New World. Spanish officials sent petitions challenging the new laws, and threatening that violence would result from the angered colonists. King Charles feared civil war might break out in his realm across the seas.

King Charles wished to reward Las Casas for his efforts to protect Indian rights. The Pope made Las Casas Bishop of Chiapa, which was an area in Central America. Las Casas welcomed the appointment because it gave him a chance to play an active role in assuring that the New Laws of 1542 would be carried out. He wanted to be on the scene of action fighting to protect the Indians.

It was a beautiful day in March 1544 when Las Casas returned home to Seville to be consecrated as Bishop of Chiapa. He was seventy years old. Members of his family and friends sat in the church waiting for the dramatic moment. Bishop Las Casas left the church that same day sailing westward to the New World. This time he did not leave Spain seeking wealth and power. He returned prepared to take on all enemies of the Indians.

Chapter 7

Bishop of Chiapa

Bishop Las Casas set sail for Central America with fifty Dominican priests. Their ship ran into bad weather and storms, causing them to lose most of their supplies. When they stopped in the West Indies to obtain needed repairs and pick up new supplies, they were greeted by hostile Spanish colonists.

"We don't have supplies for Indian lovers," said some colonists. "Why don't you go back to Spain and leave us alone. We know how to treat the lying dirty Indians." This was his first warning that many opposed the New Laws.

It took nearly a year to reach the Yucatan area in Central America. The Spanish officials and townspeople showed continual hatred toward the priests, frequently refusing to give them food or shelter. "My friends," Las Casas told the priests, "it is clear Indians are still being held as slaves. These people refuse to act as good Christians."

The Bishop of Chiapa finally reached his destination in 1545. The governor showed open hatred. "How do I know you really were appointed Bishop by the King?" he asked. "Most Indian lovers never tell the truth, so why should I believe you?"

"Your Excellency," replied Las Casas, "if you do not accept my letter of appointment, then King Charles will be directly informed of your actions. I suspect His Majesty will

Bartolome de las Casas from the portrait drawn and engraved by Enquidanos, redrawn here by Leslie Carow.

not put up with such disrespect for his authority." The Governor finally agreed to acknowledge his appointment.

A few weeks after his arrival in Chiapa, the Bishop received a letter from an angry colonist: "We say here that the sins of your land must be very great indeed, when God punishes it with such an affliction as sending the anti-Christ for bishop."

This sentiment was only the tip of the iceberg. On the Bishop's daily stroll through town, people spat at him, shouted curses or turned their backs. Little children were encouraged to shout insults. The townspeople swore an oath to remove him as bishop. Even Las Casas was unprepared for such viscious hatred.

Another and more disturbing surprise awaited Las Casas. He discovered that many members of the clergy in Central America backed the position of the colonists and officials. Many clergy had their own encomiendas and did not wish to give up their Indian slaves because they felt close to the colonists, and they wanted to protect the economic wealth of their friends.

An even worse reaction to the New Laws took place in Peru. King Charles had sent a new governor to enforce the laws. The Governor was met with open rebellion when he arrived in Peru. Rebels, headed by Gonzalo Pizzaro, brother of the conqueror of Peru, refused to obey the Governor. They defeated troops loyal to the King, captured the Governor, and refused to allow the New Laws to be carried out.

King Charles was shocked by the open opposition to his ideas. Reports of riots, rebellions, and angry protests poured in from all parts of New Spain. The colonists charged that King Charles was going back on his word. They had been granted the right to have encomiendas by prior monarchs, and now he wanted to take away these guarantees.

A whirlwind shook New Spain. Bartolome de las Casas was at the center of the conflict. A Spanish historian writing at the time said that Las Casas was "one of the most hated men who has ever been in the Indies." The storm that had been brewing in Chiapa finally unleashed its fury on Easter Sunday, 1545.

The annual Easter duty required that people go to confession and receive absolution in order to take communion. Las Casas withheld the right to hear confession from any priests who were loyal to the colonists. He demanded that slaveholders free their Indian slaves if they wished to have their confessions heard by a priest.

The town exploded in anger. Colonists shouted curses at Bishop Las Casas. Children taunted him with hateful songs when he walked in the street. He was slandered in the press and called vile names. A bullet was fired through his window. Those priests who backed him were cut off from funds and left penniless.

One priest who was closely tied to the colonists defied Bishop Las Casas and heard confessions from slaveholders. The Bishop was furious and sent police to halt these activities. The townspeople surrounded the church and refused to allow the police to seize the priest. The police retreated. "Let's get that dirty traitor, Las Casas," shouted some townspeople. An angry mob marched to the house of Las Casas.

Several members of the mob drew their swords. "Kill the traitor, kill the Bishop," shouted some men. A few officials appeared and urged the mob to calm down. The priest fled town and was excommunicated by Las Casas.

Bishop Las Casas decided to personally investigate what was being done to end slavery in the land of Tuzulutlan. He discovered that colonists were still conducting slave raids in defiance of the New Laws. His efforts to put a halt to these raids was blocked by officials. They refused to give him soldiers or any aid.

Las Casas realized success depended upon getting support from other members of the clergy. He went to Honduras to meet with clergy who were attempting to find a way to enforce the New Laws. Las Casas insisted that the encomienda system be abolished. He also wanted a new law that forbad any Spanish person from remaining in an Indian village for more than eight days in a year.

Bishop Las Casas insisted that royal officials who did not obey laws ending Indian slavery should be excommunicated from the Catholic Church. The Bishop of Guatemala opposed this proposal. He wrote King Charles: "Casas has been so arrogant since he came here as a bishop that nobody can do anything with him. He would be better in Castile in a monastery than in the Indies as a bishop."

The Bishop of Guatemala got support for his opposition to Las Casas from Alonso Maldonado who had been sent by King Charles to enforce the New Laws. It was common for officials from Spain to arrive with liberal ideas regarding Indians, but they were persuaded by the colonists to change their minds. Maldonado adopted the colonials attitude of hatred toward Las Casas. He once shouted at a meeting, "throw that lunatic out of here."

Once again Las Casas found himself isolated from any support. "I often go about alone without any layman or cleric to accompany me, because I adhere to God and to his Majesty." He abandoned hope that royal officials or the Bishop of Guatemala would give any aid to the Indian cause.

A tired and weary Las Casas mounted his horse and headed back to Chiapa with a few Indian companions. As he approached the outskirts of Chiapa, he was met by some Indians. They told him, "the colonists ordered us to wait here until you arrived. We are to tell them when you come because they wish to do you harm. Please accept our apology for aiding those who hate you."

The Bishop hugged each of the Indians. "I do not wish to have you punished for warning me of their evil plans. I will tie each of you to these trees to give the impression we overpowered you and prevented you from informing them of our arrival."

The Las Casas party moved slowly toward the city. Suddenly, there was a terrible roar. The ground shook. An earthquake hit the city causing wide spread damage. Being superstitious, his enemies immediately blamed the Bishop for the earthquake and waited to attack him.

The angry mob which confronted Las Casas when he entered the town demanded that he allow priests friendly to the colonists to hear confessions. Bishop Las Casas, realizing that things were getting out of hand, agreed to compromise. "I shall appoint two priests who favor your cause to hear confessions." Suddenly, a priest who backed Las Casas cried out: "Don't give in. Hold firm against these enemies of the Indians." A riot broke out.

Las Casas retreated to the Cathedral, the mob, with swords drawn, close behind. Bishop Las Casas was exhausted, but he refused to give in. "I allowed two priests to help you but I will not back down in my determination to protect Indian rights. Kill me if you wish and face the consequences from King Charles."

The mob leaders retreated, and decided to take out their anger on Indians in town. All night the cries of Indians being beaten could be heard. By morning, a fatigued calm settled upon the town.

The townspeople and Las Casas, totally exhausted from the constant battle, finally reached a compromise. He agreed to allow several priests friendly to colonists to hold confession; and the colonists agreed to cease attacks upon the Indians.

But a peaceful settlement was not to last for long. A few weeks later, news came that King Charles had revoked most of the New Laws. He feared civil war in New Spain. The Indians were to remain in virtual slavery.

Discouraged, but not ready to abandon his cause, Bishop las Casas journeyed to Mexico City to meet with clerics regarding the New Laws. The meeting was stormy. A majority of the clergy opposed Las Casas and supported continuing the encomienda system. Las Casas counterattacked by urging stricter punishment for slaveholders. He wanted to deny them final absolution. This idea shocked clerics.

Las Casas realized that without reinstated support from the crown nothing further could be done to help the Indian cause. He decided to return to Spain and personally argue his ideas to the king. Las Casas left Mexico in April, 1547 and headed for the court and a new fight.

Chapter 8

The Great Debate

Upon his arrival in Spain, Bartolome de las Casas went directly to the court of King Charles. He discovered a bitter argument raging among members of the clergy and royal officials about how best to treat Indians. His opponents in the clergy wanted Las Casas brought before the Inquisition to answer for his criticism of the Church and monarchy.

The King had mixed feelings about the New Laws. He was sympathetic to the pleas of Las Casas about the need for fair policies toward Indians. However, he was mindful that the great majority of colonists in New Spain were prepared to rebel if the New Laws were enforced. King Charles decided to summon representatives from both points of view, and have each present his arguments.

The group opposing the New Laws was headed by Juan Gines de Sepulveda, a philosopher and clergyman who was regarded as among the most brilliant thinkers in Spain. Bartolome de las Casas represented the side urging fair treatment of Indians.

Both men wanted Christianity spread to the New World. Both agreed that the King should control territories in the Americas. They disagreed on the way to achieve these goals. Las Casas supported the peaceful conversion of Indians, while Sepulveda was willing to use any means, including force, to convert them.

Following is a rewritten version of the debate. The ideas of both men are presented with a high degree of accuracy. Sometimes, their actual words are used; other times, modern language is employed to present their ideas.

Sepulveda:	Greetings, dear Bishop. It is a pleasure to discuss these issues with such a fiery champion of Indians.
Las Casas:	It is my honor to have such a worthy opponent. I have always admired your work and brilliance of mind. I hope you will keep an open mind about the need to treat Indians with respect.
Sepulveda:	There is no hatred in my heart against Indians. The Bible gives many examples of God commanding the Israelites to wage war against barbarians in order to bring religious truth to them. Our noble monarch acts in accordance with the scriptures in going forth to bring barbarians under the control of civilized people.
Las Casas:	Dr. Sepulveda, you are distorting the Bible. God did command the Jews to wage war, but only to reclaim the ancient land of Israel. Christ our Lord asks us to turn the other cheek, not to attack innocent people.

Sepulveda:	You call them "innocent!" How can you call people "innocent" who sacrifice one another upon stone alters? How can you call them "innocent" when they are cannibals who attack and devour one another?
Las Casas:	You speak of horrible deeds among the Indians, and what you say is true. There are cannibals among Indians. But, what about Europeans? Shall I tell you about Spanish soldiers who, for amusement, thrust swords into the bellies of pregnant women? Shall I tell you of babies thrown into rivers to be drowned? How can we who are so evil claim the right to conquer people who do evil?
Sepulveda:	The difference is that people assembled in this room know it is wrong to kill innocent women and children. We also know it is evil to refuse to end cannibalism and the worship of false idols.
Las Casas:	You speak as though all Indian nations are as one.There are cannibals among Indians, but they are a minority. The majority of Indians are peaceful. They welcomed Europeans with open hearts, they shared food and shelter, and their reward is to be conquered and enslaved. I have lived for over thirty years among Indians, and observed their skills and brilliance in the arts, crafts, and in

38

agriculture. Surely these abilities prove they are not barbarians.

Sepulveda: You admit Indians are cannibals and engage in human sacrifice. This is sufficient reason for a Christian king to take up arms and end these barbarous practices. I hope you are not telling the clergy assembled in this hall that Indians are equal in faith and civilization to Christians! God has commanded us to uplift the ignorant and bring truth to the unbeliever. We must spread Christianity even if it means evil acts are committed along the way.

Las Casas: I challenge your claim that Christian kings have the power to invade any country they desire to propogate the faith. The Indians never challenged the right of Christians to be Christians. They never attempted to seize our lands. They never displayed hatred toward Christ our Lord. Nor have they seized Christians for use in human sacrifice. How can we, as true Christians, justify attacking the innocent? Are you saying that might makes right?

Sepulveda: Your defense of these heathens indicates a lack of faith in your religion. Your support of the monstrous Indian practice of human sacrifice violates all that Christians hold to be true and correct behavior. Are you saying that you would

	stand ildly by while one Indian eats another Indian?
Las Casas:	Every pagan, however confused he may be, believes his God to be true. Every pagan, like every Christian, is indebted to God. They are willing to sacrifice human life to their gods. We cannot in a few words get them to abandon their beliefs. I believe Indians will abandon their false gods if shown through peaceful means the beauty and truth of Christianity. You cannot use force to make an unbeliever a Christian. Change must come from the heart, not because of fear.
Sepulveda:	Your ideas are shocking. You actually defend the right of these pagans to violate all Christian belief. You would stand idly by while innocent people are killed because you fear offending the feelings of these monsters. A good Christian acts against evil. You talk. I want action against unbelievers.
Las Casas:	You seek following a road leading to war and destruction. You claim interest in saving Indians from cannibalism and idolatry. But, what is the price asked of Indians in order to get the truth of our ways? Over half the original Indian population found by Columbus is dead. Millions of others endure

Juan Gines de Sepulveda, from the engraving by J. Barcelona, after the drawing of J. Maca, redrawn here by Leslie Carow.

cruel slavery. Families are ripped
asunder. Their cities are destroyed,
their temples desecrated, their crops
wiped out. You argue that this
devastation is justifiable because
the sacrifice of a few humans to
their gods will be put to an end.
What price salvation, my learned
friend, what price salvation?

Sepulveda:

I do not deny atrocities have been
committed. These were regrettable
acts. The greater good, however, is
served. Spanish settlers have
brought the word of God to
heathens. They have taught
barbarians how to cultivate the
ground and live in decency. No
longer do people walk around in the
nude. The King seeks only what is
good for his subjects. We must
continue the encomienda system
and, in time, the Indians will cease
being barbarians and be able to live
on an equal footing with
Christians.

Las Casas:

Yes, the King must do what is best
for his subjects. The Indians, also,
are his subjects. They are entitled
to protection. Slavery must be put
to an end. Missionaries should go
in peace and practice the art of
persuasion to bring the truth of
Christianity to Indians. You
cannot impose your values upon
other people through means of the
sword. The word of God is
powerful: it will triumph if only

	given the chance. Let us trust in the truth of Christianity.
Sepulveda:	I assume, dear Bishop, that if you oppose the use of force against infidels, you are against the Inquisition. Are you also saying that Jews should be allowed to practice their heresy? Are you arguing that the Catholic Church lacks the power to correct the evilness of Judaism?
Las Casas:	There is no question that Jews and Moslems have committed greater infidelity than Indians. Indians never knew Christ, therefore, their ignorance excuses them from reprimand or punishment. But, and I cannot emphasize this strongly enough, they should never be oppressed nor denied the right to work and live in peace. Jews have a right to freely practice their religion. I believe gentle persuasion and truth will eventually show them the path to Christianity.
Sepulveda:	I cannot believe my ears! First, you excuse the barbarism of Indians because they never knew Christ our Lord, then you argue for giving Jews freedom of religion! Is the Church to blind itself to evil? Is the Church to deny its obligation to bring truth to wrongdoers?

Las Casas:	I fervently believe that Jews should turn to Christ our Lord. My ancestors made that decision. But, they made it freely, not under threat of death or punishment. Christianity cannot be spread by the sword, it must come from the heart and mind of each individual. You and I seek the same end goal. We differ on the road to that destination.
Sepulveda:	It is clear we are at an impasse. You are willing to allow evil to exist, I am not. I want Christianity brought to the Indians now. I do not wish Indians to be given a choice between living in sin and living in Christianity. There is only one way for humans to exist, and that is as Christians. If it takes the sword to achieve beauty and truth, so be it. Future generations of Indians will thank us for the force we use today to prepare for a wondrous tomorrow.
Las Casas:	I agree we have reached a dead end in this discussion. I can never agree on the use of force to impose my beliefs upon another human. I know that Christianity is the true religion, but I would never wish another person to become a Christian unless he freely came to that decision.
Sepulveda:	A transcriber has kept a careful record of what each person said in

this debate. Let it be given to the King, and I trust he shall wisely conclude that Christianity should immediately be brought to the ends of the Earth by whatever means that must be used.

Las Casas:

I know that King Charles is a wise and good man. I know that he cares about the well being of all subjects in his realm, including the Indians. I am confident he will bring peace and justice to the Indians of the Americas.

Chapter 9

Fighting to the End

The great debate ended without a clear cut solution. King Charles remained uncertain about how best to handle the question of freedom for Indians. Las Casas decided he could best help the Indian cause by remaining at the court and attempting to influence the King. He resigned his position as Bishop of Chiapa, and made arrangements to live in a Dominican college located near the court.

Las Casas was seventy-seven when he embarked on his last campaign. He traveled throughout Spain urging members of the clergy to support Indian rights. He personally recruited young clerics to migrate to New Spain where they could aid Indians. His age and length of service in the Catholic Church gave him prestige, and few dared to confront his sharp mind in open debate.

It was common practice in 16th century Spain for writers to first obtain permission from the Church or King before having their books published. Las Casas broke this rule by publishing in 1552-1553 a series of articles attacking supporters of Indian enslavement. His defense of Indians took him one step further on the road to freedom for all people.

His new book challenged the power of kings to rule without the consent of the people. He argued that a king could not take land from people and give it to others. Las Casas stated that each individual had a right to be free, and that people could only be ruled by those who serve their interests.

46

He believed that if a ruler acted against the interests of people, they had a right to replace him as their ruler.

These ideas challenged the right of King Charles to rule over Indians. He also argued that the encomienda system was illegal because it violated Indian rights. This "consent of the governed" theory was similar to the one cited by American colonists when they rebelled against King George III two hundred years later. Las Casas was denounced to the Inquisition for daring to challenge the "divine right theory" under which kings ruled as though given the power by God.

The Inquisition hesitated confronting Las Casas because of his friends at the court. His personality and eloquence won over several members of the Council of the Indies. Clerics he sent to New Spain organized petition campaigns in support of Indian rights. Las Casas persuaded the King to send new officials to the Americas who were sympathetic to freedom for Indians.

He also completed the book he had begun in the 1520s. His History of the Indies was the first major work describing Spain's conquest of the New World. Fortunately for future history, Ferdinand Columbus loaned Las Casas a copy of the Columbus log which was included in the History of the Indies. The remaining copies were lost. If not for Las Casas, no record would exist of what Columbus saw on his first voyage.

Las Casas reached the age of eighty, then ninety, but the struggle for Indian freedom continued. He occupied three cells in a Dominican college. One cell was turned into a library, another into a study, and the third was his bedroom. Young priests came daily to help in the writing and organization of books and pamphlets.

His staff kept Las Casas in contact with events in New Spain. Indian oppression continued. The situation in Peru was particularly bad for Indians so Las Casas sent a special group of priests to that area to support them in the conflict with Spanish settlers.

King Philip ascended the throne in Spain. He was deeply in debt, and eager to please Spanish colonists in Peru who promised large sums of money if he would retain the encomienda system. Las Casas came forth with a counter offer. A group of Indian leaders in Peru offered a large amount of money if King Philip ended the encomienda system. He feared rebellion by the colonists and kept the encomienda system.

Las Casas renewed the attack. He openly criticised the present and past kings of Spain for sending cruel men to the New World, and supporting their policies of death and destruction. Las Casas confronted the King in person: "Your Highness, I have always been a loyal supporter of the monarchy. But, you must end this tyranny against Indians. You must give Indians their freedom and end the encomienda."

He continued writing about cruelty in the New World. His last book termed the conquistadores as "tyrants" and claimed their behavior was immoral and illegal. This was not a popular view in Spain which glorified the conquistadores.

Las Casas was ninety-two and still fighting. He wrote to Pope Pius V urging that he issue a decree forbidding war against the Indians. The summer of 1566 was hot. Las Casas felt the suffocating heat hamper his breath when he walked in town. He lay down for a nap on the afternoon of July 20th. Sometime in the midst of a dream, the final sleep came. His last will contains a summary of his accomplishments in life, and a warning:

> God in his goodness and mercy saw fit to
> choose me as his minister, though
> unworthy, to plead for all those people of
> the Indies, possessors of those kingdoms and
> lands, against unheard of and unimagined

oppressions and evils and injuries received
from our Spaniards... and to restore them to
the primitive liberty unjustly taken from
them. I say and hold it certain that all the
crimes committed by the Spaniards against
those people with such perverse cruelties,
have been against the pure and most
righteous law of Jesus Christ, and against all
natural reason, and to the greatest infamy of
His name and the Christian religion, and the
total obstruction of the faith. And, I believe
for those impious and ignominious works so
unjustly and barbarously committed God
will pour His fury and anger upon Spain if
she does not perform a great penance.

Chronology

1474	Bartolome de las Casas is born in Seville.
1492	Christopher Columbus reaches the New World.
1493	Father of Bartolome de las Casas sails with Columbus on the second voyage.
1502	Bartolome de las Casas arrives in the West Indies.
1507	The New World is named America after Amerigo Vespucci.
1511	Father Montesino urges freedom for Indians.
1514	Bartolome de las Casas decides to support idea of human rights for Indians.
1515	Las Casas visits Spain to urge Indian rights.
1522	Las Casas takes vows as a Dominican priest.
1537	He works for peaceful conversion of Indians in Guatemala.
1540	Las Casas returns to Spain to fight for Indian rights.
1542	King Charles issues the New Laws.
1544	Las Casas becomes Bishop of Chiapa and sails for Central America.
1545	King Charles revokes most of New Laws.
1547	Las Casas returns to Spain.
1550	Sepulveda and Las Casas have the Great Debate.
1566	Las Casas dies in Spain.

Bibliography

Friede, Juan, (ed), *Bartolome de las Casas in History,* Northern Illinois Press, DeKalb, 1971

Hanke, Lewis, *Bartolome de las Casas,* Martinus Nijhoff, The Hague, 1951

Helps, Arthur, *The Life of Las Casas, The Apostle of the Indies,* George Bell and Sons, London, 1896

Knight, Alice, *Las Casas, "The Apostle of the Indies,"* The Neale Publishing Company, N.Y., 1917

Las Casas, Bartolome, *History of the Indies,* Harper & Row, Torchbook, N.Y., 1971. Translated and edited by Andree Collard

Wagner, Henry, *The Life and Writings of Bartolome de las Casas,* University of New Mexico Press, Albuquerque, 1967

About the Author

Dr. Fred Stopsky is currently Professor of Education at Webster University where he previously served as Dean of Graduate Programs and Director of Teacher Education. He is co-author of *The American Experience,* a high school textbook, and has written several other books including *Freedom and Control, The Nuremberg Trials,* and a study of Father Kolbe. Professor Stopsky has been active in conducting workshops and presentations pertaining to the Columbus Quincentenary, and topics related to the expulsion of Jews from Spain in 1492. He is a member of NCSS, ASCD, and serves on the St. Louis Holocaust Commission.

52